IN THE CLIMB

IN THE CLIMB

Eight Audacious Actions to Overcome Life and Climb the Corporate Ladder with Joy

Markiesha E. Wilson

In the Climb

Requests for information should be addressed to:

Markiesha Wilson
pursuejoy@wilson-chapman.com

ISBN 978-1-7376223-0-7

Cover artwork by Saudia Jones
Cover design by Bedro Brand Box, LLC
Interior design by lindseybeharry.com

Printed in the United States of America

For my niece and daughter,
Kaijah M. Wilson, who is, was, and always
will be the joy inside my climb.

Contents

Acknowledgments

I WOULD LIKE TO HONOR my mother, Laraine Mary, and my father, Stanleigh Steven Wilson, who made me who I am, blessed me with their best traits, taught me tough lessons, and loved me with all their heart's capacity.

I would like to pay tribute to my great-grand-mother, Elizabeth Chapman, the angel who tilled the soil and paved the way for me to be a bold business-woman and fearless entrepreneur.

I wish to express my deep affection and apprecia-tion to Lynetta Carson, J. Fletcher Robinson, and Cassandra Taylor, who lit the spark and gave me reassurance to write this book.

I extend my profound gratitude to my dear friend, Jodi Wicks, who took the first look at my life story on paper and cheered me on, and to Leilani Squires, my encouraging editor and gentle guide to becoming an author.

I am forever grateful for Sandra Aljami, Lisa Dingle,

Carol Jackson-Simmonds, Krusheta Wiley, Lytonya Jernigan, Angela Course, Theresa Harrison, Dorris Powell, and Nancy NeJame who surrounded me with their support and pushed me forward when I got tired.

I would like to express my thankfulness for the many people who have, in their own exceptional way, supported my climb. A partial list includes Ambreen Baig, Chris and Kelly Bedrossian, Craig Bozzelli, Warren Brooks, Donnice Brown, Kim Brown, Michela Calhoun, Lindzey Capri, Mike Charles, Keisha Chase and the Chase family, Cynthia Cleckley, Glenda Crest, Bernard, Dawn, Randl, Iysha, and Kendall Dent; Sherrie Eaton, Keira Edwards-Perry and the Edwards family, Marc Glascoe, Leontyne, Derrick, Saudia and Elijah Jones; Andre Joyce, Brian Leak, Marlene and Josette Kelley, Heather McDaniel, Debra Loreilhe, Hanif Aljami and the McMillian family, Tracey Morton, Nikita and Sara Nazarenko, Cherie Nelson and the Bigger Splash crew, Lisa, Greg, Jada, and Gavin Newton; Ed Offerdinger, Cassan Pancham, Vernita Parker, Josef Passley, Tanya Perry, Michelle Roberts, Melissa Robinson, the Robinson family, Loleta Ross, Matt Seipp, Michelle, Marjorie, and the Shelton family, Haritha Shematek, Jackie Smallwood, Angela Smith, Britni Smith, Cynthia Smith, Robin Steele, Bishop Walter S. Thomas and the New Psalmist Baptist Church Family, Erik Thompson, Lisa Tsyvine, Yolanda Vazquez, Voris Vigee, Blair and Deidra Wilson.

By Joi Thomas

Author, Playwright, Radio Host, and CEO of Joiful Communications

WHEN WE ARE YOUNG, we watch with curiosity and excitement as those older than us navigate life. We see all the perceived glitz, glam, and freedom and imagine what it will be like when it is our turn. We follow the prescribed path and get our high school diploma, and in most instances our college degree and even master's and doctoral degrees. We get married and have children and it seems that we have achieved the main goals in life that every one sets out to accomplish. However, life is not that simple.

As you get older, you begin to see what the adults didn't always share when you were younger: Life is unpredictable. Rarely does it go as planned. One thing can lead to another and suddenly you find yourself on a different path you didn't plan to take.

What do you do when life is harder than you bargained for? What do you do when you don't have the energy to create a new plan?

The answers to these questions can be found right here in this book by Markiesha Wilson. She has lived through this and, with God's help, has found a way to still be productive, happy, and successful even when her plans changed. *In the Climb* reminds us that we are all human, living life the best we can. It gives us insight on how to explore the opportunities presented to us and make the best out of them. It offers a blueprint on how to use disappointment as a way to learn more about yourself and your relationship with God.

I am especially excited about this book because I have known Markiesha for over thirty years. I have seen her successes and failures, her high moments and moments of pain. It is always hard to see friends deal with calamity, but it is so rewarding to see them overcome. Markiesha has made it and now she is helping others see that same success in the workplace.

In the Climb will remind you of all the wonderful traits God gave you and how you can use them to overcome any challenge life presents. This book will motivate you to keep going. Climbing anything takes a lot of focus and strength. It is highly likely that you will get tired and want to give up. It is in those moments that this book will be of most help.

Workplace struggles can be a source of contention. Plans can be thwarted and corporate battles can wear you thin. Markiesha offers hope and strength for anyone going through professional struggles. Your career may be important to you but it does not define who you are. This book will help you find purpose beyond a job, which will help you fulfill your purpose.

Allow the words of these chapters to penetrate your soul and give you the strength and clarity you need to keep climbing. Allow them to fill you with hope and give you permission to dream again. Most importantly, allow them to reassure you that you are on the right track and to keep climbing!

Chapter 1

Envision Possibilities

If we desire to reach our destination of greatness, we will need to envision possibilities.

"WHAT IS POSSIBLE FOR ME?" is a tough question we need to ask often. For many of us, it can seem unrealistic to imagine a reality different from the one we live today and reaching new and better heights.

Many of us have lived with limiting belief systems for so long we don't believe we can accomplish life's essential tasks, let alone greatness. Whether these beliefs come from our parents, friends, teachers, or nosey neighbors, we accept some small picture of our future. Looking forward to a future where only the sky is the limit is liberating. But how do we step forward, with our eye on the prize?

To succeed, despite our circumstances, we have to diligently battle negative thoughts and change our speech. We often believe our dreams and goals are impossible to achieve because of numerous reasons. We were born in this country, state, city, neighborhood, family, gender, and skin without our choosing. We didn't choose the hardships we face. Or something said by someone we trust causes us to doubt amazing things can happen in our lives. But, in some cases, we self-sabotage with our own words and thoughts.

If we're not careful, our past will keep our minds trapped into thinking there's no reason to believe for more. I was born into a middle-class Black family of entrepreneurs. I grew up in a large four-bedroom house in the Philadelphia suburbs, with a pool in the backyard and a grocery store below. I was also born into a family which endured the pain of ugly divorces, untimely deaths, unacknowledged alcoholism, and undiagnosed mental illness—a family of widows, divorcees, and mothers who buried their sons, daughters, and emotions. I could easily have fallen into the trap of believing my life was destined for these adverse circumstances.

But at fourteen years old, I started to learn about God. This was not a God who punishes for petty crimes, but a loving God who cared about me and wanted the best for me. This changed my view of everything. I spent many years getting to know God, hiding from Him when I wanted to "do my thang," and running back to Him for protection after my actions caused problems too big for me to solve on my own. I learned God sees me and my future possibilities from a totally different view. He protects and provides for me because His plan for my life is way bigger than any mistake I could ever make.

To see my life as God planned for me, I had to get close to Him—right next to Him. When I get close to God through prayer and reading the Bible, or listening to sermons, I can see the positivity despite my negativity. Praying did not stop the hard things going on in my life, but it stopped limiting my focus. I could focus my vision on our family's pool parties instead of family feuds and funerals. Talking to God and asking Him to show me the way forward to greatness is how I have learned to see what is possible for my life.

Monitoring what we consume while endeavoring to reach greatness is another way to shift our perspectives and open our minds. I am amazed at how much time people spend on social media and binge-watch awful news and then seem surprised to realize their outlook on life and their future is jaded. Consuming negative things will cause us to feel more negative.

Consuming positive things will help us feel more positive. Clearly, we must stay aware and connected to what is happening globally. Social media serves that function exceptionally well while also opening our minds to discover new possibilities. However, we should also know how much we can honestly handle without being overtaken by negativity.

With the advances of modern technology, all we could ever want to know can be found with a few keystrokes on our favorite device. When discontent coworkers and clients ask me for advice about finding passion in their work, I say, "Google what you really want!" An internet search can reveal what is possible. It was a simple internet search that changed my whole life in March of 2006 when a nor'easter blizzard hit Maryland.

This blizzard kept us locked in the house for two weeks—something unheard of before the 2020 COVID-19 pandemic. At the time, I worked for a financial institution that allowed us to work from home. I was on a call with colleagues, developing a training course, when I declared my disgust with winter and joked I should move to St. Thomas, U.S. Virgin Islands. For years, I had traveled there for vacation. While still on the phone, I searched the internet for "jobs in St. Thomas." Among the search results I found my dream job: training and development officer at a bank in the Virgin Islands. I thought it was too good to be true. My eyes were opened to the possibility and I could not unsee myself living a dream.

But I couldn't leave Maryland—not when I was helping my mom raise my late sister's son and daughter. I couldn't consider pursuing my happiness when my mom was miserable with health issues and being a full-time single parent again. I couldn't follow some lofty idea when I was the breadwinner for two households. No way. I did not have the confidence to move forward, so I told myself to just close my eyes and pretend not to see this perfect path to joy.

And I prayed. I asked God for signs to assure me. That's when things started to happen.

A friend knew someone who worked at the bank. What could it hurt to make a few friendly phone calls? I called Carol, the bank's vice president of Human Resources. I said I'd be on the island in a few weeks and would love to have lunch. It was a lunch of succulent grouper served with a side of delightful conversation. As I flew back to Maryland, I was sold on landing my dream job.

Many weeks passed. Because I had not heard anything about the position, I gave up hope. Then one day, a colleague who attended one of my trainings and recalled my love for St. Thomas told me she had just landed a job at a bank in St. Thomas. My heart dropped. Did this chick take my job? What are the odds this would happen? Is this a sign? But no, none of my assumptions were true. She had gotten a job at a competitor's bank.

As soon as I got back to my desk after our conversation, I had a missed call from Carol. Breathless, I called right back. She said they loved my background and I was well qualified. But, unfortunately, my salary was way out of their range. I listened feeling sad and punched in the gut. I had come too far in prayers to believe it was supposed to end right here. I asked what the job would pay. Two days later, I received a FedEx package with an offer $30,000 less than my current pay. After a pep talk with my mom, who said it was a terrible idea to give up my six-figure income for this stupid dream, I called Carol and accepted the offer. And the rest is *herstory*.

The journey to greatness is not a short, smooth, clear path. It is a long, rough road with stretches of limited visibility. If we desire to reach our destination of greatness, we will need to envision possibilities, encounter possibilities, endure negativity, exercise generosity, embody audacity, explore creativity, exemplify tenacity, and finally, embrace serenity. Achieving greatness requires accepting periods of abundance and famine while knowing our Heavenly

Father has divinely equipped us to handle both.

Achieving our greatness is, in fact, possible. We must open our minds enough to believe what we see as impossible today is possible tomorrow when we take the proper steps toward it.

ENVISIONING POSSIBILITIES @ WORK

Sometimes we fall into dark periods at work as well as in our personal life. This is when we struggle to see new career possibilities and only see the clock telling us to stay at the desk for more hours.

These dark periods may be because you have performed a role for some time and are ready to move on. But you may not know where to begin to figure out what is next. One way to discover what other possibilities exist at your current place of employment is to ask your leaders for additional work assignments. Why on earth ask for more work? Because if you are exposed to new opportunities, then you have more possibilities. This can open doors for the work you desire but may not know is available. When you are succeeding in your role, and then ask for more responsibilities, it is highly likely to be given to you. This also enables you to have more interaction across teams within the organization, which leads to more networking and meeting leaders who have access to other positions and roles you could pursue.

"If you can?" said Jesus.
"Everything is possible for
one who **BELIEVES**."

Mark 9:23 (NIV)

When you realize you cannot grow further at your current company, then it's time to expand your vision. A simple first step is what I did: run an internet search using a few keywords that resonate with the work you want, not necessarily job titles. For instance, if you are looking to use your oral communications skills and love to travel to the tropics (like I do), search for public speaking and the Caribbean. Searches reveal organizations and professional events within the fields you may want to pursue. Running the search may not always yield a long list of vacancies. Still, it may open your eyes to possibilities you did not know existed.

When you find a job that piques your interest, begin identifying what requirements you need to acquire before updating your resume and pursuing it. Then, when you're ready to apply for these desired roles, saying "yes" to every interview is the next step. Even if you aren't interested in an exact role, the conversations and connections can steer you toward the dream job.

God promises a life of abundance, peace, and joy to those who believe. Let's see what's possible for us when we dare to believe and get brave enough to take a step forward.

Take Your Step

ASK YOURSELF

What is possible for my life and career?

TASK YOURSELF

List three things that bring you joy and can invest your time doing.

Herstorical Fact

MADAM C. J. WALKER was born in 1867, right after the Emancipation Proclamation. By age seven, she had lost both parents. To survive, Walker worked as a domestic servant for several years.

She envisioned a better life for her and her daughter, so she took a job selling hair care products. After a long time working at her dream with her unstoppable persistence, she was able to build a house, a factory, laboratory, hair salon, and a beauty school. Walker became the first self-made female millionaire when women were not expected to be much more than housewives.

Becoming a millionaire was impossible for a woman, especially a Black woman, until Madame C.J. Walker paved the way. While becoming a millionaire may not be your goal, Walker's life is an inspiration and model for steps we can take when we look at seemingly impossible goals.

Just like Madame C.J. Walker did, challenge yourself to envision possibilities and a better way of life and then move toward it with all your strength.

Chapter 2

Engage Opportunities

Dreams are accomplished by engaging in the opportunities that come our way.

I BELIEVE DREAMS ARE God's way of getting His work accomplished on earth. God gives us dreams to bring about His master plan. As His plan unfolds, opportunities are presented, which lead us to fulfilling our dreams—but only if we engage in them.

I am a dreamer. Since childhood, I have spent hours escaping into a world I created where everything was possible. As a teenager, my dreams included meeting Michael Jackson, winning an Oscar, studying law at the Paris-Sorbonne University in France, and becoming the president of a university. None of these have been fulfilled and one is impossible now (though I do pray MJ made it to heaven to moonwalk down the streets of gold).

These dreams didn't come true not because they were unrealistic, but because I never took steps toward achieving them. Dreams stay dreams while we are asleep—but to accomplish them, we must wake up and get to work. Dreams are accomplished by engaging in the opportunities that come our way.

Many people have dreams but struggle to achieve them. They talk for months, years, and even decades about waiting for the right time, or for when they'll have enough money, or when their kids grow up, or when they retire. The list of unexcused absences from reality is endless. If you are serious about your dream, the practical process (shown below) is to move from a dream, to a goal, to a plan, to an action, and then ultimately to reaching achievement. This takes both work and time to prepare yourself holistically in every way possible—spiritually, financially, and physically.

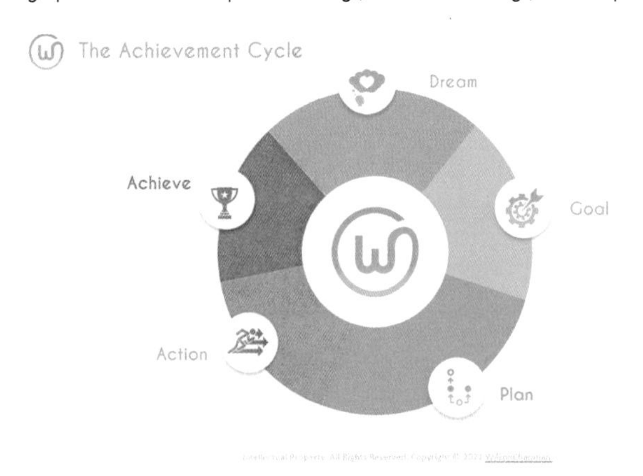

In my roaring twenties, I did not realize the need to move through all the levels of preparation. I thought I could just dream it and with the right amount of hard work, connections, and faith, it would happen. This belief is one of the downsides of being a woman of great faith. Sometimes, I have skipped the planning details step and just taken leaps of faith, trusting God to do the miraculous. It looks super holy to people, but I have learned it is foolish at times. It's not that God can't move miraculously, but rather God moves strategically.

Every single thing God created was crafted with precision. Scientists are still trying to figure out how God's creation works. What took God only seven days to whip up is still baffling humans thousands of years later. God has a plan and so should we.

To prepare spiritually to pursue dreams, begin with prayer. God made each of us to serve a unique purpose only we can do. So, doesn't it make sense to ask Him what that purpose is? I admit I have skipped or improperly executed this step more than once as well. I dreamed and moved forward without asking if it was God's perfect will for my life. Spending time in prayer by just talking to God in our own words brings us closer to achieving our dreams.

Dreams cost. If there is anything we want to do tomorrow that isn't being done today, we need to find ways to fund it. Unless you are in the top 10 percent of Americans and considered wealthy, you will have to save some money and prepare yourself financially to achieve your goals. If you are in that top 10 percent, see Chapter 4 on generosity, because there are people in need of your excess abundance. Dreams need funding to be executed.

Often, when God gives us dreams to do something specific, it is strategically intertwined with someone else's dream. In those times, we are divinely connected by God, which allows both of our dreams to come to true and accomplish His plan.

A first step in running after your dreams is to eliminate debt. This can be done initially when you stop buying unnecessary things. Chances are we do not need more shoes, a new designer bag, or a brand-new car to keep up with the Jones's.

MY STORY

At thirty-two, I decided to pursue my dream of entrepreneurship. I had been working at a well-respected management consulting firm and was stressed out. I believed I had learned enough to step out on my own. I was praying and looking for signs. One day, we had a large team meeting with a motivational speaker. As I watched him, I knew that was exactly what I wanted to do.

My manager, Debra, came to me at the end of the speaker's presentation and said she could picture me on stage as a motivational speaker. There it was: a divine sign from God! A few months later, I was in my director's office resigning from my position.

With no plan and no savings, I stepped out on faith. Surprisingly, I was able to make it from famine to feast a few times over the three-year period. But eventually, I needed to return to the good old nine-to-five for stability. There were family challenges, which led to that decision, but had I planned a bit more, I may have been able to stay independent longer.

Fifteen years later, I decided to engage my entrepreneurial opportunity again. This time was different. When I decided to start WilsonChapman™, I was older, wiser, and full of bought lessons. I knew to carefully plan because the stakes were much higher. My niece now relied completely on me for her livelihood and the sting of those financial famine days were not far away in my memory.

I wanted to be an entrepreneur from the time I had to take a full-time job and provide a stable lifestyle for my family. The desire never went away, but I knew I had to wait. Raising my niece was my priority. Making sure I gave her the best rest of her childhood mattered more to me than my desire to call my own shots and count my own profits. I stayed in corporate America longer than I ever wanted to because I had to. I left three different positions I loved to have a schedule that allowed me to take my niece to school and leave in time to see her play soccer or dance at church. I loved my niece so much more than those jobs. I knew my time would eventually come for me to live my dreams, but only after I had handled my priorities.

But I did not wait idly. For a solid two years, I planned every detail, task, cost, risk, dependency, and milestone deadline with precision.

MY SETBACK

But I never thought about how I would accomplish my goals as an entrepreneur if I got ill. Unless you have been sick, preparing yourself physically for your dreams is often an overlooked step. It is said an ounce of prevention is worth a pound of cure. Getting our bodies in the best condition to take on opportunities is essential. Without good health, you are unable to get much of anything done. Health isn't something you can buy. Even the richest people could not buy themselves a cure for their illnesses. Steve Jobs, the pioneer of Apple, with all his wealth and intelligence, could not for any price get a cure for the illness that took his life.

I confess I spent almost no time working on living

a healthy lifestyle. I took for granted that I was blessed with good health. But, all this changed when I was forty-eight and got sick. I was used to slight stomach discomfort, so I didn't pay attention when it was getting progressively worse. For days, I suffered with sharp pains in my abdomen. But I kept working hard and running here, there, and everywhere. Then, one day, I could not ignore it anymore. My stomach felt like a gremlin was inside trying to claw his way out. I could not walk and was in my bed, cringing. It was then I decided I should go to the doctor. Bright idea, but pretty late.

The doctor said I needed a CT scan, which I never had before. After some tough-love coaching, from my friend Mike, to drink the barium, I was in the tube holding my breath and fearing the outcome. I was diagnosed with diverticulitis, a very painful gastrointestinal disease. That was the day I started to pay attention to my health.

The pain was hard to handle, but treatable with antibiotics. I was lucky I caught it early enough to avoid surgery. The problem was I had many deliverables due on my current project and I was still trying to build my new coaching business. I did not have time to be sick.

Lying in bed, in pain, fear took control of my mind and stopped me from doing anything productive.

I laid there fearing the worst—a surgery that would leave me with a colostomy bag. And the only bag I want to carry around with me all the time is a Chanel! Then the what-ifs invaded my mind like persistent White House reporters barraging me with probing questions: What if you get sick when you start your business? What if you can't make money? What if you get the contract of your dreams and can't fulfill it because you're sick? What if this is a sign from God that you are to stop pursuing your dream right now?

Fear is powerful. A popular acronym for FEAR is False Evidence Appearing Real. It was not easy to fight those thoughts and fears. I knew I needed God to help me get through this. I started praying for healing and strategies. The strategy and answers came. I found a nutritionist, started asking my doctors more questions, and pushed to get additional tests. I learned you must advocate for yourself to get the healthcare you are paying for. I pulled myself together and started to pursue a healthier lifestyle. I researched proper diets for GI conditions, started exercising more regularly, and listened to podcasts.

Healthy living was new to me, and I needed to learn from as many sources as possible as quickly as possible. I know there are thousands of health plans available everywhere. Taking clear steps to follow a plan that aligns with your physical needs and health goals will give you the energy to pursue promising possibilities that come your way. Health is wealth.

Taking time to prepare ourselves enables us to engage in opportunities when they appear. If we can find as much time to plan as we do to dream, we will be better positioned to complete the necessary steps to move from dreams to goals to plans and, ultimately, to achievement through our actions.

ENGAGING OPPORTUNITIES @ WORK

Project planning is not the most exciting task, however, it is necessary. No matter how large or small the project is, a detailed plan is necessary in order to execute it effectively and efficiently.

I learned how to masterfully manage people, resources, and time while working at a management consulting firm. One of my managers, Haritha, was a driven project management guru with high standards for quality and low tolerance for inefficiency. Haritha introduced me to the value of planning out every task in a spreadsheet, for which I am grateful. As we worked on large-scale implementations of training and change-management projects, she taught me how to plan for risks, client changes, resource challenges, and even contract loss.

The discipline of documenting everyone's responsibilities served me really well as I sought to create my

"**COMMIT** to the Lord whatever you do, and he will establish your plans."

Proverbs 16:3 (NIV)

second business. I created lists of tasks, added due dates to them, then updated the status as steps were completed.

Creating plans keeps you on track and moving from your dream, to goal, to plan, to action, to achievement. Spreadsheets were also my compass for getting my business up and running. To create my business, I used the spreadsheet below:

MILESTONE	TASKS	DECLARATION	GUIDING SCRIPTURE/ QUOTE/AFFIRMATION	DEPENDENCIES	DUE DATE	STATUS	NEXT STEPS

When planning, dump everything you know you need to do in a simple spreadsheet. Include every single task you can think of initially and then figure out when it needs to be done. Order accordingly. Sometimes, it works best if you start at the end goal and work your way backwards. This can be especially helpful if you have a goal launch date, or a deadline.

The plan serves as a compass on days when you don't know what to do next and can help prevent you from feeling overwhelmed. Planning the execution is as important as dreaming the dream, if not more. Resisting the urge to skip steps and details is the best way to engage in opportunities and transform dreams into realities.

Take Your Step

ASK YOURSELF

What dreams and opportunities have I avoided pursuing?

TASK YOURSELF

Identify the opportunities to engage in and begin to fill in the spreadsheet with attainable tasks. Choose an accountability partner for support.

Herstorical Fact

HARRIET TUBMAN is perhaps one of the most strategic executors of plans in history. Harriet, also known as Black Moses, conducted more than a dozen trips over an eleven-year period to lead slaves from Maryland to freedom in Philadelphia. Having carefully orchestrated three thousand known conductors of the Underground Railroad, she carried out her dream of freedom for herself, her family, and many others despite the extremely harsh realities she had to endure.

Harriet Tubman's life is a shining example of how dreams can get fulfilled, regardless of the hardships, when plans are executed in reality.

Chapter 3

Endure Negativity

No matter how many powerful people hurl negativity at you while you pursue your goals, you can keep stepping forward and accomplish them.

NEGATIVE PEOPLE AND SITUATIONS are unavoidable. To thrive in your career and find joy in life, enduring negativity will become necessary during some part of your journey.

For me, enduring negativity started as a child. My mother was not a mommy type who doted on her children and showered them with love, affection, and compliments. She was a divorced, single mom with a command-and-control mentality. She ended her directives to my brother, sister, and me with, "Do it immediately, if not sooner." There were no two-way conversations, just linear lectures.

My mother did not have anything kind to say to me. She never told me I was beautiful, intelligent, or destined for greatness. Instead, she told me I was born a girl because my father did not deserve a boy. The absence of positivity caused negativity, just like the absence of light is darkness. However, as a responsible provider, my mother made sure she dressed me in clothes that made me feel cute and sent me to great schools to become smarter.

I started kindergarten at the age of four because my mother taught me to read well at home. I still remember my first day of school. I was so excited to wear my brand-new Winnie the Pooh dress straight from Sears. My first school year progressed, and I thought everything was going fine. I even completed my math workbook early with the help of my sister. Reading group was the best part of my day because I loved learning new words, and recess was my least favorite because I feared making new friends. Just as the school year ended and I was getting ready for first grade, I found out I had to go to summer school.

"Oooooh, ooooh, you're dumb," my sister, Jackie, teased.

Jackie was older than me by three years and she found many things to tease me about. I was too skinny, too dark-skinned, and too buck-toothed. She took great pleasure in teasing me all summer, and for years to come, about how dumb I had to be to flunk kindergarten.

I knew my sister was kidding, and though her words still hurt me, they paled in comparison to the treatment coming from my mother. My mother was from the old school where beating your children was how you disciplined when they did not do exactly as they were told.

I worked hard to get my chores done before my mom got home from her second job, but I still got yelled at and beaten with a brown leather belt. Back in the late 1970s, my friends got spankings, too, but my mother was different. She had a very short temper and would become enraged for seemingly no reason and beat me for extended periods. She would scream mean things at the top of her lungs and do strange things to punish me for something I never did. When I was six years old, she burned my stomach with her cigarette because she thought I was looking at her with disrespect. My mother had zero tolerance for any behavior that remotely resembled disobedience. Back then, it seemed like the physical abuse was causing me the worst pain. Now I believe her negative words hurt me more, even though I still have that scar on my stomach.

To survive my mother's unpredictable behavior throughout my teen years, I prayed to God and read the Psalms every day. I could understand the scriptures and believed God would protect me from the pain at home. Day after day and year after year, I got closer and closer to God. I knew He was the only one listening to me and answering my prayers. I prayed about everything that happened at home and at school, primarily tests I did not study for and cute boys who did not notice me. I knew God heard my cries for help because I felt strengthened when I prayed and was able to do well in school despite what was happening at home.

All through school, my mom expected me to get the best grades in our household. And I did. School was always my escape from home life. When I was there, everything made sense. I worked hard and was rewarded with good grades. Teachers complimented my outgoing personality and my classmates laughed at my silly jokes. I was even voted “Most Humorous” of my senior class. Education was critically important to my mother, so it was important to me.

I got straight A’s almost every year except eighth grade when I became obsessed with Michael Jackson. As the youngest of three, I was eager to do everything my brother and sister did. I worked hard on my schoolwork, thinking I could catch up to them somehow. Believing they thought I was dumb, I worked diligently every school year and all the way through college.

I was determined to prove to my sister and everyone else who underestimated me that I was smart. I completed my bachelor's degree with honors, and without missing any parties on the East Coast. A few years later, I finished my master's degree with a 4.0 while working full-time. Ironically, this was when my mother finally explained I was asked to go to summer school after kindergarten because I needed to develop "social skills." Social skills! Because I frequently turned down recess and playtime with my classmates to get my math workbook done, my teachers figured something wasn't quite right with me. Wait, what? All those years, while working so hard, I thought I was dumb. And no one told me otherwise? I couldn't believe it!

As I reflect on those hard, formative years, I realized I didn't know the way my mother talked to me was wrong or unhealthy. It seemed normal because my grandmother spoke to and about my mother even worse. I can't remember hearing a single complimentary statement from my grandmother about my mother. Nor do I remember my mother saying anything positive about my grandmother. I believe our family suffered from this mother-daughter curse for three generations.

For me to heal, it took years of prayer, counseling, self-discovery, and distance. When I left for college at seventeen, I had endured all the negativity I could handle and I never lived with my mother again. Our complicated relationship had few highs and many lows. As an adult, I can understand my mother suffered from some undiagnosed, unacknowledged, or untreated mental illness. I knew my mother did the best she could with the tools she had to use.

ENDURING NEGATIVITY @ WORK

When negativity is normalized at home, I suppose it's easier to deal with outside of the house. Whether that is right or wrong, I believe that's why I was able to endure negativity in the workplace. Webster's dictionary defines endurance as "the ability to withstand hardship or adversity, especially: the ability to sustain a prolonged stressful effort or activity."[1] It was exhausting to work in consulting firms heavy-laden with crabs climbing on top of each other to get to the top, sly silver foxes digging holes for their competitors, gorillas beating their chests demanding alpha male status, and flocks of little birdies full of gossip flittering about everywhere.

To survive without losing myself, I learned to prepare for each day and focus on my end goal. I kept positive quotes at my desk and in notebooks to glance at and remain calm during meetings when the gorillas started beating their chests. Some days,

"You, Lord, hear the desire of the afflicted; you **ENCOURAGE** them, and you listen to their cry."

Psalm 10:17 (NIV)

I failed miserably and ended up in the office parking garage napping at lunchtime to fight off the migraine caused by the madness. Other days, I spent time in preparation with prayer and affirmations. In 1928, Florence Scovel Shinn wrote *Your Word is Your Wand*, and offered this affirmation, which helped me stay positive in the workplace: "I am poised and powerful; my greatest expectations are realized in a miraculous way."[2]

Creating your own affirmations can also be a powerful and freeing exercise to fight off negative thoughts at work.

The list of negative workplace issues is extensive. We have all lived, or at least heard about, being passed over for a promotion when we knew we earned it; not making the same salary as our colleagues; someone else getting the credit for our ideas; being interrupted and talked over; and more. When this happens, we can complain to the Human Resources office, throw tantrums, or quit and hope it doesn't happen again at a new company where the grass looks greener. (Note: The grass may be greener at the new company, but it is fertilized with, shall we say, the same stuff.)

When I started the EnterTraining Group at thirty-three years old, I had mastered the ability to endure negativity by working in demanding companies that were not inherently supportive of women or people of color. I was asked to deliver a motivational training to a workplace team, which I called "Walking Up the Down Escalator." I talked about how I managed to be successful despite the negativity I had faced as a Black woman in corporate America. I explained how working in a negative environment is like trying to walk up the down escalator. Every force in the office is on a downward trajectory—all the energy is dark, dreary, and dragging you down. But I had to succeed. I had to prove that, no matter the odds, I would not let the escalator take me down.

When we find ourselves in places where processes, people, policies, and politics are pushing us downward, it's time to push back. Here are five ways to do so:

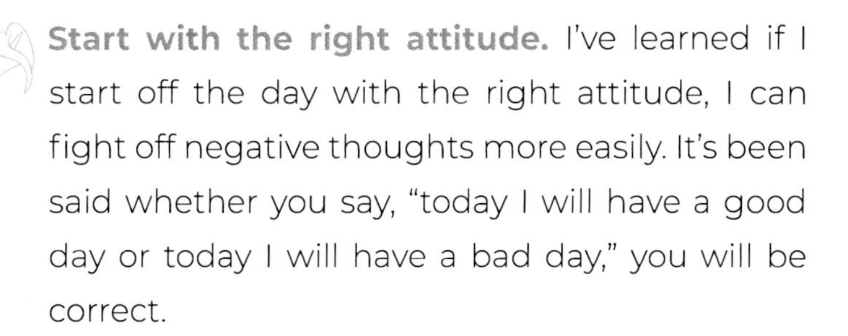

Start with the right attitude. I've learned if I start off the day with the right attitude, I can fight off negative thoughts more easily. It's been said whether you say, "today I will have a good day or today I will have a bad day," you will be correct.

Watch your mouth. Watching what you say to yourself and to others is critically important. Proverbs 18:21 says the power of life and death is in the tongue. When we are in heated workplaces boiling over with contention, our words can either heat up or cool down the situation. The best choice is to take on the role of the ice cube.

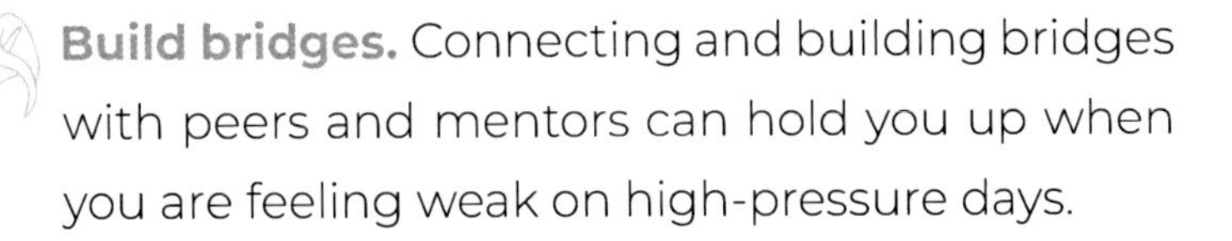

Build bridges. Connecting and building bridges with peers and mentors can hold you up when you are feeling weak on high-pressure days.

Sync up. Strategically connecting with managers and leaders can enable you to see the big picture and shine a light on possibilities you can't see because you are too close to negativity.

Climb up. Catch your balance, dig your heels in, and start climbing up the corporate ladder one baby step at a time. When your focus stays fixed on your dream goal, it can be easier not to be engulfed in the negativity surrounding you.

Take Your Step

ASK YOURSELF

Who or what negative force is in the way of my success?

TASK YOURSELF

List three steps you can take to minimize this negative impact.

Herstorical Fact

AT SIX YEARS OLD, Ruby Bridges faced and endured negativity for trying to do something so basic—go to school. Ruby was the first child to desegregate a formerly all-white school in the south on November 14, 1960. On her first day at William Frantz Elementary School in New Orleans, she had to walk past an angry mob of white people protesting her attendance.

To protect Ruby and her mother, the United States president sent four U.S. marshals to escort her into school daily. As she arrived, more than two hundred protestors shouted cruel words and threw things at her. They threatened to poison her while marching around the school, carrying a coffin with a Black doll inside. Every day, Ruby faced the same crowd of parents who did not want their children attending the same school because she was Black. Because of this, Ruby had to be taught in a classroom all by herself. But Ruby was a courageous young girl and endured the hatred and went to school every day. In the early 1990s, Ruby volunteered as a parent liaison at William Frantz Elementary School. Today, a statue of Ruby stands in the courtyard.

The story of Ruby Bridges reminds us that no matter how many powerful people hurl negativity at you while you pursue your goals, you can keep stepping forward and accomplish them. Ruby also models the power of returning to the place where you endured negativity to infuse it with your newfound positivity. That's what walking up the down escalator looks like.

Chapter 4

Exercise Generosity

If you give away everything you need,
it will come back to you when you need it most.

I STRONGLY BELIEVE THAT to achieve the success we are after, we must be generous. And if we are open to giving away what we need, it will come back when it's needed most. Generosity is vital, personally and professionally. Whether it's time, talent, advice, or money, giving is a practice we can incorporate in how we live.

Being a Black woman, I have always wanted to give back. I am confused by successful people, especially women, who are not willing to reach back and bring the next generation of women along with them to success.

My first professional job after college was as an assistant director of admissions for Towson State University. I was so proud to work for my alma mater and for a Black woman who was the director of admissions. I was twenty-one years old, working a job with my own office, secretary, and American Express card. Do you know you can charge anything on that card? Did you also know you are supposed to pay the full balance every month? A critical financial lesson learned the hard way.

My job responsibilities included recruitment in predominately Black areas and high schools. I drove the state-issued Chevy Cavalier for recruitment trips to New York's boroughs and throughout Baltimore and Prince George's County, Maryland. My goal was to increase the minority enrollment of the incoming class, which hovered around 10 percent. It was a personal goal to encourage Black students to go to college. I would deliver my presentation on the university's benefits while highlighting aspects Black kids in the nineties cared about then: co-ed dorms with 24-hour visitation, job placement rates, phones in every room, and bathrooms only shared by two roommates. At the end of every presentation, I would launch into my three key points just like every good speech and sermon should: plan, prepare, and pursue.

- **Plan:** figure out what is out there and get organized to go after it.
- **Prepare:** get ready by getting equipped.
- **Pursue:** go after it actively with all your heart.

Afterward, I closed by saying it does not matter if you choose to attend Towson or not, but please go to college. I quoted Malcolm X: "Education is our passport to the future, for tomorrow belongs only to the people who plan for it today."[3] I spent time with every student and helped them fill out applications. I waived fees and I personally took calls from students who were nervous about their SAT scores and grade point averages.

I remained committed to students once they arrived on campus. I helped get them jobs, took them to the grocery store, and even housed a couple over summer breaks. I encouraged them when they wanted to drop out and supported them when their white professors had not learned how to be sensitive to their unique needs as underrepresented minorities. I was generous with my time and used my position to support every student I could as they pursued their education.

Generosity has always been a core value of mine. But I did not know why until I completed the discipleship program at the New Psalmist Baptist Church (NPBC) in Baltimore. For three years, I studied my role in God's divine plan and how He uniquely equipped me with spiritual gifts. Spiritual gifts are supernatural abilities given to Christians by the Holy Spirit to get God's work done in our lives and others.

On Wednesdays, I left work like the building was on fire to get to Baltimore by 6:30 p.m. from Northern Virginia. This can take anywhere from one and a half to four hours, depending on weather, accidents, and drivers on cell phones. It was worth it because I was learning so much about God, who I was, and in the company of eight other women who became lifelong friends—the kind of friends who show up or call for every joy or sorrow.

In the second year, we completed the spiritual gifts assessment. After several questions, the results were in and confirmed my gifts as giving, teaching, encouragement, and faith. It was then, at thirty-two years old, I came to understand how God hard-wired me to give, teach, and encourage others to believe in God even in the toughest of times.

There are several personality assessments you can take to identify your core strengths and tendencies. For another layer of self-awareness, I also encourage you to take a spirit-ual gifts inventory to help identify which you are equipped with for your divine purpose. Some scholars say there are as many as eighteen spiritual gifts. *The Spiritual Gifts Inventory* is accessible at LifeWay Christian Resources.[4]

For me, the spiritual gift of giving goes beyond holidays, birthdays, and special occasions. It is activated whenever I see a need. I've paid for groceries, meals, and clothes for strangers who were fumbling at the register with that familiar look of lack on their faces. In my late twenties, my mother was ready to buy her first home as a divorcee and needed help with the closing costs. I immediately volunteered to give a few hundred dollars, which felt like a few million in those days. But I was so happy to give back to the one who had provided for me. The next day, just as church started, I crouched in the pew to call my automated bank line and check my balance and determine what I could still afford to put in the offering basket. Yes, I know my giving priorities were out of order. After my gift to mom, four of my own checks bounced and my account was in the negative more than $500.00.

As my pastor, Bishop Rev. Dr. Walter S. Thomas, Sr., gave the morning announcements, I sat there with a pit in my stomach. How could doing something right cause me such problems?

No good deed goes unpunished, I thought.

Then Bishop Thomas asked a random question, one I'd never heard him ask before or after in all my thirty-four years of membership at NPBC. "Who is going to close on a house this week?" he asked.

I nearly fainted. My mother's closing was scheduled for Wednesday. I cried as my mother and two other women stood up. In a sanctuary that sat about 1000 people, only three women rose. He asked them to walk to the altar.

"Is there anyone who is praying for a house?" Bishop Thomas said. "If so, come and sow a seed to help these women get theirs. We will divide all you bring amongst the three of you, and the church will give you each additional money to help you."

As my mother and other ladies walked to the front, people came to the aisles to give a seed offering. That day, my mother received more than twice what she needed for her closing costs. I bought the video of that church service so I could see over and over again how it really happened. If you still have a VCR, I can show it to you. That Sunday, I learned God is a generous Father who will supply all His children's needs. And I realized my mother was God's daughter, just like I was hers.

My lessons continued in 2004 when my sister, Jacquelyne, suddenly died of a heart attack at age thirty-five. I loved my sister very much, and though we weren't always besties, the unresolved distance between us was now permanent and made her unexpected death all the more painful. My mother and I stepped in to raise my eleven-year-old nephew, PJ, and four-year-old niece, Kaijah. This decision was made without a second thought and obviously without a second to plan anything—not even for the emotional or financial impact this would have on us. About six months prior, I had started my first human resources consulting business, The EnterTraining Group. As other small business owners can attest, it is feast or famine. And I was definitely in a famine, both emotionally and financially.

To make matters more challenging, my mother was not able to work due to her many knee surgeries. I gave her everything I could. I paid her mortgage and mine, bought clothes, covered family vacations, furniture, and even purchased her a Toyota Forerunner.

A few days after my sister passed away, I spoke with a friend, who I call "The Bridge." I call him that because back in college, whenever I caught a glimpse of him walking across the bridge from the dining hall to the Union, my heart would skip a beat. He hails from the same New York borough as The Notorious B.I.G., Jay-Z, and my alter-ego Lil' Kim. As The Bridge and I talked about losing my sister and becoming an instant parent, he asked what I needed. I responded

"Each of you should give what you have decided in your heart to give, not reluctantly or under compulsion, for God loves a **CHEERFUL** giver."

2 Corinthians 9:7 (NIV)

with my standard firm Black woman answer, "Nothing. I'm okay. No, really, I'm good."

The Bridge had been a friend for over two decades, so he knew better than to believe my automatic response. A few days later, the doorbell rang. There was a FedEx package containing a beautiful sympathy card and a check for several hundred dollars. About an hour later, the doorbell rang again. This time, the Baltimore Gas & Electric company came to collect the past due balance or turn off my electricity. My heat and lights stayed on.

What I learned was if you give away everything you need; it will come back to you when you need it most. However, I also learned I am not always supposed to give. I still give whenever I can, but now I say a prayer first to make sure I should. I give because I know how it feels to be in need and now I am blessed to have plenty to give.

GENEROSITY @ WORK

Demonstrating mentorship, sponsorship, and allyship are wonderful ways to exercise generosity in the workplace. Sure, you can give awards and compliments at work to exercise generosity. However, the gift of knowledge and support can have a more prolonged and meaningful impact. Giving your valuable time to mentor junior level employees at your company can be the greatest act of generosity.

Whether your company has a formal or informal mentorship program, you can offer your insight to new people on your team. If you are in a leadership role, or have seniority, consider actively becoming a career mentor. Simple steps are outlined by a fellow Accenture alum, Sheila Downer-McCoy, in *Shape (Strategically Help Another Person Elevate)*.[5]

- **Prepare** yourself to be a mentor.
- **Commit** the time to your schedule.
- **Identify** someone you can and want to help with your experience.
- **Contact** them and co-create a regular schedule to meet.
- **Listen** to their concerns.
- **Share** your story, including successes and failures.
- **Offer** practical suggestions.

Sponsoring someone's elevation in an organization is another way to exercise generosity. Sponsorship is bringing someone physically or verbally to the table who otherwise wouldn't get an invitation to attend.

At another management consulting firm, Lisa, a super-smart self-assured Sicilian, was my leader, mentor, and sponsor. I marveled at her ability to remain authentically and unapologetically herself whether she talked to her clients, peers, direct reports, or senior partners. Her example of such genuine girl-grace freed me to display the same. As I worked alongside her, I became more and more comfortable being funny, flirtatious, and frank, as needed.

Lisa strategically ensured people above me and her knew my name. When I told Lisa I wanted to attend Georgetown University for the Leadership Coaching Certification, she sent emails, made phone calls, and used her role to position me and make it happen. Two years later, when I told her I wanted to leave the firm and become a subcontractor, she sent emails, made phone calls, and used her influence to position me and make it happen then, too. That is giving the gift of sponsorship.

I have looked to women throughout my career for encouragement and empathy on my journey as I try to break through the glass ceiling, which caused them concussions and dream damage. These women shared the dos and don'ts of the organization, pushed me to do more than the rest and get on leadership's radar, and were beacons of light on dark days when I doubted myself.

Because of experiencing this kind of generosity, I strongly recommend you choose at least two mentors. One mentor should look like you in age, gender, and race, and the other should look as different from you as possible. Mentors who have the most in common with you from a demographic perspective may relate to your experience more. Those who are different can provide unique experiences to guide you in ways you would not be aware of necessarily.

As I built professional relationships with older white men at work, I realized they were happy to help guide and share information with me I would never have been privy to otherwise. I have avoided plenty of pitfalls in business because I was willing to quiet my own unconscious bias, face my fears of vulnerability, and accept advice from those who looked nothing like me. As a result, my career has flourished even in the most unlikely organizations and times.

For my melanin-free friends, allyship is a selfless act of generosity you can exercise toward your colleagues of color. Allyship became a commonly used term in the summer of 2020 after the murder of George Floyd. This unarmed Black man was murdered by a police officer who chose to press his knee into George Floyd's neck until he died. The Black Lives Matter movement helped uncover how allyship can show up in many forms. According to *Harvard Business Review*, allyship is viewed as a strategic mechanism used by individuals to become collaborators, accomplices, and co-conspirators, who fight injustice and promote equity in the workplace through supportive personal relationships and public acts of sponsorship advocacy. Allies endeavor to drive systemic improvements to workplace policies, practices, and culture.[6] Allyship is truly about taking the time to learn about race, systemic racism, and how to look out for the best interests of historically oppressed people. Being an ally is using the power of white privilege to position someone of color and give them the gift of support in the workplace.

Most people spend more time complaining about problems in our communities, countries, and world than giving of ourselves toward the solutions. I am certain I would not be where I am personally or professionally if people did not step up to give me what I needed. I urge you to consider helping someone who could benefit from your time, finances, wisdom, or support. If you can find ways to share your intellectual or professional capital with someone more junior, you will be giving an impactful gift.

Take Your Step

ASK YOURSELF

Who do I know who needs something I have?

TASK YOURSELF

Contact them and give them what they need within 30 days.

Herstorical Fact

IN 1939, MARIAN ANDERSON, the internationally acclaimed contralto, made history. Because of First Lady Eleanor Roosevelt's sponsorship and allyship, Marian sang to seventy-five thousand people on the steps of the Lincoln Memorial and to millions via the radio.

The world-famous singer was previously denied the opportunity to sing at the Constitution Hall, which was owned by the Daughters of the American Revolution (DAR), because she was Black. Eleanor Roosevelt was so outraged by the institutionalized racism displayed by the organization that she chose to resign her membership from the DAR. Eleanor Roosevelt made arrangements for Marian to perform at the Lincoln Memorial. As Marian sang "America" to the world, First Lady Eleanor Roosevelt smiled with pride.

Another First Lady, Michelle Obama, was a mentor to a bright young lawyer named Barack at a Chicago law firm. History books around the world proudly record how successful he became because of her mentorship!

These two examples, again, show how supporting and giving of your time, resources, and influence can turn the world upside down. But what is also inspiring is how these two ladies gave their attention—they noticed what was going on around them. They saw individuals, what they were going through, and acted in ways that brought about more good. This is something everyone can do, no matter the financial or success status.

Chapter 5

Embody Audacity

Audacity is a critical component of change.

EACH YEAR, MILLIONS OF self-help books are read, thousands of sermons preached, and numerous inspirational quotes are posted on social media. These messages aim to drive us to live our dreams, take better self-care, set appropriate boundaries, and take leaps of faith. Unfortunately, most of us never even take the first step. Why? Because being bold and taking risks is scary.

The word audacity comes from the Latin word "audacitas" which means boldness. Often, the word carries a negative connotation, likely because of the two parts of its definition. The first part defines it as a willingness to take bold risks. The second defines it as a rude or disrespectful behavior. Perhaps this is why we hear a ticked-off tone when people say someone had the audacity to do this or that thing we think is inappropriate. In my experience in corporate America, when we are judged as too young, too female, or too tan, there is a tendency to describe confident, clear statements or stands as audacious. It's as if there is a line we dared to step over or we haven't "stayed in our place," then we are labeled audacious.

The Cambridge Dictionary captures the essence of why I believe embodying audacity is an essential step toward thriving in life. It defines audacity as "showing too much confidence in your behavior in a way that other people find shocking or rude."[8] History shows how what others found shocking, or rude, actually propelled societies to progress beyond their antiquated beliefs and behaviors. Audacity is a critical component of change.

Working in high-performing environments often means working with and for Type A personalities who are ambitious and driven. In those places, I had to decide whether to shrink or stand tall. I admit there were many times when I surveyed the room and saw giants who seemingly could not be defeated. So, I sat in silence, even when I knew the answer to the question or the best solution for the client. I sat silent because I was afraid I would be talked over, shut down, or ignored. More times than I would like to admit, I softly stated my idea only to have someone else repeat it verbatim, but with confidence, and take the credit as if it was theirs. Many times, I went to the ladies' room to collect myself.

I eventually got tired of holding my breath and literally biting my tongue to keep calm. I was tired of looking in the mirror and knowing I was just as smart, if not smarter, than the giants in the room. I was tired of feeling afraid to step up and be visible. Just plain tired. I decided I was done cowering in corners. I was going to say what I thought regardless of the reaction. While I would like to say I consistently prepared for my nervy moments, often I just blurted out my thoughts and erupted with remarks because I was totally over it. Hindsight being 20/20, I believe consistent preparation for these kinds of interactions would have enabled my moves to be more strategic and I would have fewer regrets.

When I was thirty-five, I landed my dream job leading the training organization for a financial institution in the U.S. Virgin Islands. In my first month, I was invited to the executive leadership team's weekly meeting. However, I was not an executive. There I was at my first meeting, looking out the window at the turquoise water, hardly believing I was there.

As I listened to a conversation surrounding the employee engagement survey results, a debate started about who was the proper person to deliver the message to the employees. Some shared their concerns that the senior leader would not be the best choice because he may be perceived as "intimidating."

"Intimidating?" I said under my breath with a slight Philly girl attitude.

"What did you say?"

Oops, he heard me, I thought.

My manager looked down and hid her face in her hands. But I sat up straight and cleared my throat.

"I don't know why anyone finds you intimidating because I do not," I said. I also said I'd be happy to assist creating the presentations to deliver the message effectively to the employees.

Whoa, that was bold, right?

Surprisingly, the senior leader agreed employees should not find him intimidating and he was happy to be the one to deliver the message throughout the organization he cared for so deeply.

That audacious act opened the door for me to work directly with the leader on critical initiatives and helped form an excellent working relationship. Later, he became my best business mentor ever.

As I grew in my confidence and experience, speaking up became somewhat more manageable. Sitting in meetings, I would fight off the devilish discouragement and force myself to speak up when I knew the answer. At first, I stammered out disclaimers like "I don't know if I'm using the right words or not, but..." or "I'm sorry, but..." Eventually, with pep talks and Pepto for my nervous tummy, I stopped avoiding speaking up for myself.

EMBODYING AUDACITY @ WORK

Embodying audacity is a process. It first requires building our confidence and then preparing to make the bold move. Without confidence, it can be hard to take a risk—terrifying to even consider taking a chance. That was the situation I was in as I tried to decide the right time to resign from my position.

At age forty-nine, I made a bold move and started my second consulting firm, WilsonChapman™ and Associates. But this time, I prepared. Some said launching out on my own in the middle of the COVID-19 pandemic was not wise. Yes, it was risky for sure. However, I knew leaving my job was a risk I was ready and willing to take.

I always knew I wanted to be an entrepreneur ever since I watched my great-grandmother run our family's grocery store, Chapmans. I just wasn't sure when the right time would come. I didn't know how to be sure I was taking the right step at precisely the right time. I needed guidance from God and more prayer before I would have enough confidence to move forward.

Before I could be fearless in the natural realm, I needed to be proactive in the supernatural realm. I started praying bold prayers about my future, praying for courage and asking God to guide my thoughts and words to come out clearly. I stated the promises of God and asked Him to open doors. Though there are thousands of promises in the Bible, I have learned you only need to grasp a few of them at a time to feel encouraged. Throughout my trials, I have repeated this promise:

Proverbs 3:5–6 (NIV): "Trust in the Lord with all your heart and lean not on your own understanding; in all your ways submit to him, and he will make your paths straight."

My second step was to prepare mentally. I would rehearse for challenging conversations in front of the mirror. For example, "If he says _____, I will say ______," and so on. Then I would give myself pep talks on the way to work. I started driving to work listening to powerful gospel songs like "Power Belongs to God" by Hezekiah Walker. On other days, I blasted "Fight the Power" by Public Enemy through every speaker on high. Both had me inspired and hyped up to be bold and audacious.

As a leadership coach, I share these experiences when I hear clients share all the reasons it's not the right time to make a significant move in their careers. Some reasons have merit, and some are more audacious avoidance. Many will say they lack confidence to speak up and take bold risks. Fighting off fear is hard, but without forward progression, we become stagnant.

I share those fears and have paused my own progress on more than one occasion. But my fear of stagnation is more significant than my fear of risk. I have come to learn that risk is the cost of freedom. Now I tell my clients to "be more you, more often, and more boldly."

When we learn we are capable and equipped for challenging moments, we can embody audacity. Saying affirmations, preparing, getting support from wise people, and knowing your strengths can all provide confidence to take bigger bold steps.

Discovering our strengths by taking personality assessments such as DISC, Myers-Briggs Type Indicator, and Strengths Finder provide research-based data to enhance self-awareness about capabilities and information to make practical changes to our behavior. This can help you intentionally leverage your abilities to communicate with confidence and influence and motivate others.

Seeking the support of others, such as leaders, peers, mentors, and coaches can help build your boldness muscles. When going into new or unfamiliar situations at work, having a prep conversation with someone with more experience gives you the push to say or do something you might be unsure about. In many cases, mentors have been where we are. They can share real-life perspectives on how our bold step may be received based on the people and politics involved. For some, the individual practice is needed to increase confidence. Having a certified coach to work through challenges can provide results. Through powerful questions, focused conversations, and exercises, coaches can pinpoint unknown behavior patterns preventing us from feeling confident enough to take bold risks.

Taking bold steps at work requires fine-tuned interpersonal skills to be successful. Building emotional intelligence (E.Q.) can go a long way toward building the skillset. E.Q. is so critical to success, it accounts for 58 percent of performance in all types of jobs. The four skills that make up E.Q. are self-awareness, self-management, social awareness, and relationship management. In *Emotional Intelligence 2.0*, authors Travis Bradberry and Jean Graves state E.Q. is your ability to recognize and understand emotions in yourself and others and to use this awareness to

"Do not be anxious about anything, but in every situation, by prayer and petition, with **THANKSGIVING**, present your requests to God. And the **PEACE** of God, which transcends all understanding, will guard your hearts and your minds in Christ Jesus."

Philippians 4:6-7 (NIV)

manage your behavior and relationships. Individuals who improve these skills are much more confident in social situations and therefore feel more confident to take risks and make mistakes. They have a keen understanding of how to do well, what motivates and satisfies, which people and situations push our buttons, and how to strategically choose when and how to make bold moves.[7]

Take Your Step

ASK YOURSELF

What goodness is waiting for me once I take this risk I've avoided?

TASK YOURSELF

Identify a technique to build your confidence then select a date within the next 30 days to take one baby step toward the bold step.

Herstorical Fact

KAMALA HARRIS, Vice President of the United States, was harshly criticized for speaking up for herself during a debate. As Vice President Pence interrupted her sixteen times throughout the debate, she boldly challenged him multiple times. With a cool, calm, and collected tone, she said, "Mr. Vice President, I'm speaking. I'm speaking." Mr. Pence continued to talk until she finally said: "If you don't mind letting me finish, then we can have a conversation."[9]

Her critics said she had the audacity to ask him to stop talking, insinuating she was rude and disrespectful. Kamala Harris previously had dared to run for president of the United States. Though she did not win the Democratic Party's nomination, Harris became the first highest-ranking female official in United States history and the first African American and Southeast Asian person to hold the office of vice president of the United States.

During her acceptance speech, she thanked President Joe Biden for having "the *audacity* to break one of the most substantial barriers in our country and select a woman as his vice president."[10] Her unprecedented victory confirms what Laurel Thatcher Ulrich believed: "Well-behaved women seldom make history."[11]

Chapter 6

Explore Creativity

When you are in a creative mindset,
you can open your mind to what is possible,
and not be limited by what already exists.

WHEN MOST PEOPLE THINK of exploring their creativity, they envision having to drag out crayons, scissors, or paint to create some masterpiece. But, creativity comes in many forms—and even people who don't consider themselves to be creatives could take some time to explore these avenues. Robert E. Franken in *Human Motivation* defines creativity as: "the tendency to generate or recognize ideas, alternatives, or possibilities that may be useful in solving problems, communicating with others, and entertaining ourselves and others."[12] Creativity helps you see things from different perspectives and to become a better problem solver at work and home.

Finding ways to intentionally be more creative is necessary and worth it. Why? Because your clients, co-workers, and companies require innovation. Business leaders, owners, and consultants should know today's clients are not impressed with last year's solutions.

Hairstylists and barbers, for example, are aware their clients do not want last year's haircut and style. Incidentally, if you have hair or can buy some, changing hairstyles is a simple way to practice being creative. Most women are exceptionally skilled at this, especially Black women. But I spent years being afraid to wear my hair in any other style than jet black and bone straight to ensure I looked professional. I remember being so nervous about wearing braids to work that I told my co-workers repeatedly I was just doing it for vacation. In 2021, that's a thing of the past. When you see a brown beauty boss with braids in a boardroom, no one even dares to stare. Now, I wear braids every chance I get, whether I'm headed to the Caribbean or not. To me, my braids convey creative power.

When you are in a creative mindset, you can open your mind to what is possible, and not be limited by what already exists. Finding areas of your life where you can express your creativity will give you an outlet to be free from constrained thinking. We all need a break from the mundane tasks of work and life. Immersing yourself in an activity that allows your mind to drift into your ideal happy place can be all you need.

Have you ever lost yourself while creating something and hours passed without you realizing it? Maybe you felt like you were in another world—a world where you could be you, let go, and live in the moment. Some call this being "in the zone." It's the look you see on the faces of musicians as they create improv jazz. Eyes closed, head bobbing, and lips pursed. What can you create that takes you there?

For me, acting catapulted me to my happy place. In college, we had to complete three credits in fine arts. Since I can't draw anything grander than a stick figure and can only dance well to old school hip hop, I decided to take Improvisational Theater 101 for my easy A. After a couple of exercises, Professor Doster noticed improv came easy for me, so he offered me a slot in the Towson State Catalyst Theater Company. I initially declined, primarily because I didn't want to be associated with those artsy people. But when my professor mentioned travel and pay were included, I was in!

Our group traveled to high schools and colleges in Maryland and Virginia and performed sketches about realistic situations plaguing students in the

1990s, such as homophobia and racism. Once we got snatched off a high school stage for being too realistic and potentially inciting racial violence in the crowd. When I was on stage, I would become the character—losing myself in the character's issues, mood, and perspectives. Almost in a trance, I couldn't even see the audience, just my six-foot co-star, Glenda, as we spontaneously created dialogue and actions impeccably timed for the moment. I still hear the audience's laughter as I stood on my tippy-toes at four-foot, eleven and a half inches to chastise her with my pointed finger in her face for not "acting Black enough."

After college, I volunteered to act in church plays to have an outlet from my stressful jobs and because I firmly believe we are supposed to give our talents back to God who gave them to us. I was privileged to be cast in a variety of plays written by Joi Thomas, the leader of the church's fine arts ministry. I played a racy reporter, a wife in strife, and my number one shero Harriett Tubman. I was cast as Jesus's mother so many times I almost started to believe I miraculously had a son. The acting wasn't just an outlet to me, it allowed me to open my mind and gain empathy to see and solve complex problems carefully through the lenses of different people.

Back at the office, I would incorporate this same creativity when dealing with clients and co-workers.

Spontaneously creating unique solutions for my client's complex problems opened lots of doors for me in competitive work environments. My improvisational skills enabled me to succeed because I could respond with witty words to condescending compliments in classrooms, offensive outbursts in conference rooms, and microaggressions by melanin-free folks.

As I climbed my way up the corporate ladder, the practice of cultivating creativity has served me well as a tool for innovative solutions and as a beautiful veil over my righteous indignation.

EXPLORING CREATIVITY @ WORK

Let's be clear, corporate America requires, values, and promotes creativity in individuals and leaders. However, it can be intimidating to figure out how to be creative in the workplace.

Consider intentionally scheduling play time for your mind to start your day or wind down. For busy professionals in demanding careers, the thought of sitting around thinking may sound like a waste of time, but it is actually time well spent. Opening space in your mind can expand your ideas.

Other ways can be to take on a DIY home project. The process of imagining a beautiful space in your home and creating it with your own hands can be energizing. Remember when you played a musical instrument in middle school and pictured yourself playing it in front of sold-out arenas? Try picking up that instrument again and practice playing a song or two. If you once loved to draw, buy a sketch book and doodle as you enjoy your dessert or favorite beverage. Cooking, baking, and gardening are also fulfilling ways to express your creativity. The key is to grant yourself time to dabble in creative activities.

For some, creativity comes naturally, like those who were able to knit their own booties from birth. However, for others, it's a struggle at times. Take heart, my friends! Creativity is a skill you can learn. To create free time and space to discover your creativity, try to:

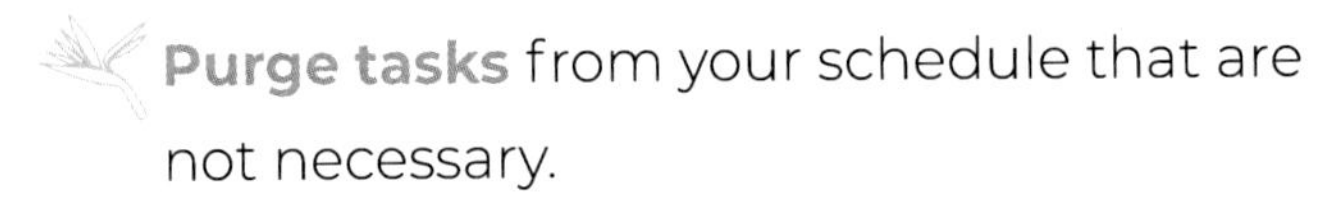

- **Purge tasks** from your schedule that are not necessary.
- **Reduce the number** and duration of purposeless recurring meetings.
- **Let your mind wander** while you move your body by walking, running, biking, or dancing.
- **Drown some tension** by soaking in a tub or swimming. Water creates a calming effect and generates creativity.

"Each of you should use whatever gift you have received to serve others, as faithful stewards of God's **GRACE** in its various forms."

1 Peter 4:10 (NIV)

- **Take breaks from social media** to increase your free time to be creative.
- **Avoid binge-watching** someone else's creativity at work.

If you lead a team, consider these techniques for enhancing your team's creativity:

- **Share your own** good and bad ideas often.
- **Establish brainstorming** sessions as the first step for work.
- **Encourage your employees** to work alone and in groups.
- **Let the team try out their own ideas** but with a safety net.

Exploring your own creativity can open many opportunities you wouldn't otherwise imagine. Consider spending time on activities that you might not necessarily think of as creative such as gardening, Sudoku, learning different languages, bird watching, roasting coffee or even doing dot-to-dot books to expand your thinking. Regardless of how you choose to cultivate it, you will discover how much enjoyment being intentionally creative adds to your professional journey.

Take Your Step

ASK YOURSELF

What is preventing me from being more creative at work?

TASK YOURSELF

Write down one activity you enjoy doing. Put time on your calendar to do it this week for 30 minutes.

Herstorical Fact

CICELY TYSON was a woman who used her creativity in audacious ways. Over her fifty-year acting career, she was known for only choosing to play resilient Black women who were thriving even while living under pressure. Tyson said, "I wait for roles first to be written for a woman, then to be written for a black woman. And then I have the audacity to be selective about the kinds of roles I play."[13] Her refusal to play roles that demeaned Black women caused her to be out of work periodically. However, she still achieved numerous accolades including Emmy awards, a Tony award, an honorary Oscar, and the Presidential Medal of Freedom.

A trendsetter for fashion and hair, Tyson showed her creativity when she wore cornrows in the movie *Sounder*, and in a short-lived television series called *East Side/Westside*, she wore her natural un-straightened hair. For this, she was dubbed "mother of the afro." Tyson's nuanced way of portraying powerful Black women with realistic subtleties broke boundaries for Black women. She played famous, strong Black women such as Harriett Tubman, Coretta Scott

King, and mothers of Rosa Parks and Wilma Rudolph. In addition, her portrayal of fictional characters, such as Miss Jane Pittman and the mother of Kunta Kinte in *Roots* illuminated Black womanhood. It allowed white audiences to secretly stare at the complexity of the Black female experience in America.

Cicely Tyson passed away on January 28, 2021, at ninety-six years old. Another queen of creativity, Shonda Rhimes, known for her creation of highly addictive television shows such as *Grey's Anatomy*, *Scandal*, and *How to Get Away with Murder* summed up the loss of Cicely Tyson in one sentence: "Her power and grace will be with us forever."[14]

Chapter 7

Exemplify Tenacity

Our ability to be tenacious
will largely dictate if we make it or not.

THERE WILL BE OBSTACLES along the way to accomplish our goals, so our ability to be tenacious will largely dictate if we make it or not.

My official college transcript records my completion of a Bachelor of Arts degree, cum laude, in three and a half years. But that accomplishment came with my share of ups and downs academically and socially, including failing Accounting 101 because I was distracted learning about college dating instead. That F grade was the only one I ever received.

On the social scene, I saw the sorority exquisitely dressed in salmon pink and apple green and my eyes lit up. However, when they smiled back at me, I heard my internal voice say, "Don't do it because you will fail." I was concerned my decision not to pursue this desire would disappoint a dear friend of mine, Safiyyah (Arabic for "sincere friend"), who was one of the leaders of the organization. Yet, I was more afraid I would have flashbacks from my childhood if the pledging process got intense. So, I gracefully bowed out, explaining I had the opportunity to graduate early and that was best for me. After I decided neither sororities nor dating were going to lead me to success, I buckled down with my academics. I took more than fifteen credits every semester and spent long hours in the library.

I had to finish college and get a job. I worked hard like my life depended on it—because it did. There was absolutely no way I was going back home to live with my mother. I had tasted freedom from being controlled, criticized, and chastised without cause.

I fought distractions and finished college without ever learning anything about accounting or how to date. I did learn sincere friendships are built by saying yes and saying no. For me to thrive, I had to say a lot of no's to people, places, and things I wanted to say yes to. In doing so, I could create the space for the things I needed to do. There are only twenty-four hours in each day, and I have learned to use my waking hours judiciously.

Fighting for my academic future was just the beginning of my training to hold on no matter what. Fifteen years later, this training and tenacity would be needed again for my career and family situations.

When I left my position in higher education, I decided to hold on to my tenacity and vision of becoming a well-respected businesswoman no matter what. I fought my own insecurities as I presented training to engineers with MBAs from Ivy League institutions. I feared my undergrad degree from a public college and a master's degree from Howard University, a Historically Black College or University (HBCU) wasn't as good as theirs. I would give myself pep talks as I commuted around the Washington D.C. beltway: "Yes, Markiesha, you know everything you need to know. You are just as smart, and you deserve to be there."

Sometimes I would disagree with myself, and God would always drop into my thoughts to break up the argument before the negativity beat the positivity. I held onto God's promise in Hebrews 10:35 (NIV): "so do not throw away your confidence; it will be richly rewarded. You need to persevere so that when you have done the will of God, you will receive what he has promised." I stayed close to God. I watched preachers before I went to work. I put up words of wisdom and affirmations at my desk to keep myself motivated to stay in the struggle. In those tough years, I was also inspired by Safiyyah, who was now raising her voice in the education arena and insisting on equity for all children just like her civil rights activist grandparents did. I had the privilege of watching her lead as school principal and gracefully respond to racist remarks at a Parent Teacher Association meeting with confidence in her eyes, a smile on her face, and stilettos on her feet. I knew I too could endure the negativity I was facing and I knew I had to make it in corporate America.

Surviving and succeeding in those high-stress places came at a cost. I had to be a lot less tenacious and a lot less Markiesha to fit in and move up. I realized this when my master's thesis advisor came to take me to lunch. After waiting a few minutes for me in the corporate headquarters lobby, he later told me, "You don't belong here. This place will kill your spirit." I knew he was right, but I was determined to fight and keep it from happening. And I did it. I made it to management in three out of the five top consulting firms in the world. I was legitimately a success. However, I failed to do it as Markiesha in my twenties and thirties.

When my sister died, my niece and nephew lived primarily with my mother. It did not take long for me to see this was not going to work long term. I watched my mother start to treat Kaijah the same way she treated me and my sister as children. My nephew did not receive the same treatment, just like my brother did not.

I knew I had to step in before the treatment got worse. After attempting to get my mother to let Kaijah move in with me full time, I realized I was going to have to involve the legal system. My stomach still aches when I remember seeing Wilson v. Wilson on the courtroom door. Thousands of hateful words, thousands of anxious thoughts, thousands of tearful prayers, and thousands of dollars later, I won custody of my niece.

As a single parent, I fought for Kaijah, and sometimes against her, to get good grades. I changed jobs to be able to work eight hours and still prevent her from being the last kid picked up from aftercare. I resigned from one leadership position because the senior leader commented that people who only worked forty hours per week were not respected. It was hard each time I left a position, but I was clear about holding on to what was most important. My number one priority was being the parent Kaijah needed. I did my best to invest my time into giving her the best present and future I could.

On a day when the pressure was getting to me, a colleague encouraged me by saying: "As a parent, the days are long, but the years are short." It was true. It seemed like one day, I was picking up Kaijah from aftercare as she carried her Dora the Explorer backpack and had four ponytails in her hair. The next day, I was picking her up from her dorm as she carried four bags of laundry and tossed long box braids over her shoulder. Parenting is the hardest job I've ever had. The tenacity it demands is abundantly rewarded in the pride I feel when I hear her speak with confidence and see her walk fearlessly toward her greatness.

I am not sure if it was my age when I reached my forties, or being a parent, or if I just got tired, but I regained my tenacity when I realized I'd had enough of the navy blue and black suits, fake smiles, and working fifty-hour weeks so I could take a vacation and be my true self on an island for five days and four nights. Why couldn't I just be me—smart and funny and an unapologetically Black woman? One day, I decided I was going to be me, come what may. I had achieved enough promotions to leadership roles. I didn't need any more awards or bonuses or kudos emails. I just wanted to be free to be Markiesha. So, I did. Little by little, I made more jokes more often, wearing more braids, and speaking up more. This is when I started to love my work.

EXEMPLIFYING TENACITY @ WORK

Here are the top ten practices that worked for me in various work environments and may help you as you implement tenacity into your workplace

- **Bloom where you are planted.** Sometimes you have to stay where you are and find ways to stand out. Often, we want to go somewhere else to be successful, but often we are avoiding the hard work staring us in the face.
- **Plant pictures of positivity** around you to keep you motivated about what matters. Whether it's a picture of someone you love, a car, a beach home, or all the above, choose something that makes you smile and reminds you of your purpose for working so hard.
- **Make peace of mind your priority** by deciding to reduce the amount of confusion, stress, and resentment you allow to rule your mind. When confusion clouds your mind, pause and spend some time searching for clarity.
- **Never say anything to yourself** that you would not say to a child. Speaking negatively to yourself can kill your motivation, focus, and will to pursue your goals. Speak to yourself the same way you would to encourage a child to do their best.

"Consider it pure joy, my brothers and sisters, whenever you face trials of many kinds, because you know that the testing of your faith produces **PERSEVERANCE**."

James 1:2-3 (NIV)

- **No is just a referral.** Each time you hear a no, be certain that it is pushing you toward a yes.
- **Stand up for** what and who you believe in. Supporting others will pay off when you need someone to support you through a tough time.
- **At the end of the workday,** forget the worry and stress and what happened. If you stay in yesterday's conversation, you can't get ready for tomorrow's.
- **God's timing is perfect.** He's never a millisecond early or late. Wait on Him to reveal what you need to do in all situations.

Take Your Step

ASK YOURSELF

What dream or vision do I still have that I stopped fighting to achieve?

TASK YOURSELF

Start making a plan to pursue your dream or vision.

Herstorical Fact

PATRISSE CULLORS, Alicia Garza, and Opal Tometi founded the Black Lives Matter movement after an armed white man was acquitted for the murder of Trayvon Martin, a seventeen-year-old unarmed Black young man. As civil rights activists, these women face criticism from every angle, yet they tenaciously hold to their vision. No matter what opposition they have faced, they push forward to fight against systemic racism, police brutality, mass incarceration, and prejudice of every type. They are also fighting to support Black men and women, especially the most marginalized, such as those who are transgender or have disabilities. Although similar movements have fought for these same rights, at present, the Black Lives Matter movement is the largest in the world.

These women model how to unite and fight passionately for what and who we believe in regardless of the odds. Standing up for those who cannot stand up for themselves can be difficult to do alone. However, joining forces with like-minded individuals who are passionate about the progress of people can make a powerful impact on generations to come.

Chapter 8

Embrace Serenity

When we avoid opening up to deal with pain from the past out of fear of future hurt, we can lose the opportunity to experience serenity.

THRIVING IN OUR CAREERS and finding joy in life requires a lot of work, but we must also find rest and peace along the journey. It's not healthy to run this race without taking time to relax our minds and care for our bodies.

Living in a peaceful state is beneficial to our overall health and well-being. Countless diseases, conditions, and ailments have been linked to living a stress-filled life. More medications are prescribed for health conditions related to stress than any other. Americans, in particular, are the most medicated society on Earth.

Yet, we know there are numerous ways to avoid stress. There are books we can read, gyms we can go to, pastors and coaches and counselors and therapists we can talk to, and even apps we can download on our over-used cell phones to help relieve and better handle stress. The Bible promises we can have peace more than 300 times—we just have to ask God for it. But even with all these tools, tips, and techniques from TV therapists and well-intentioned friends, it is still hard to find peace of mind. The COVID-19 global pandemic showed us what happens when a whole world loses its vices for stress relief. So why is it so hard for us to find peace and serenity?

To get peace in my life, I had to accept lots of things I did not want to accept, forgive a bunch of acts I did not want to forgive, and have an attitude of gratitude instead of a just a bad attitude. When I did not, I ended up with physical ailments from head to toe for years. Migraines, neck pain, back pain, and stomach issues were persistent and consistent. I could not figure out how to get peace from the stress of working full-time and being a graduate student, or from working full-time and being a single parent, or from working full-time and being a disconnected daughter.

Peace of mind is hard to find because it often requires we face things we have been avoiding. Facing hurt from the past can rob us of peace and productivity if we don't deal with it. I remember times when I was supposed to be creating a complex training course or strategic communication plan for a client, but I just could not focus. My mind was so clouded, and all my creativity was blocked. When we avoid opening up to deal with pain from the past out of fear of future hurt, we can lose the opportunity to experience serenity.

For me to experience a sense of calm, I eventually had to deal with my complicated relationship with my mother. Nothing in me wanted to do that. Even after wise counsel from my pastor and therapist, I still was not ready or willing to set boundaries even though I knew it would lead to emotional freedom. Years went by and I sent cards for every single special occasion and holiday and almost never received any acknowledgement. After all that time, I still did not get brave enough to set boundaries. Then one day, I was out of time.

On February 20, 2020, my mother passed away. Up to her death, she did not want me to know she was severely suffering from congestive heart failure. Even with all the pain I endured from her in the past, the finality of her being gone was even more painful. I was deeply hurt she specifically stated she did not want to see me before she died and to just inform me after she was gone.

As I prepared for my mother's memorial service,

I sorted through the feelings I had been holding. My nephew did not ask me to speak or do anything for the service. But I wanted to be ready, so I prepared a speech. Memories rushed in, some really bad ones and some really good ones—from my crazy childhood, to college conflicts, to the cold custody battle. From our sunny beach trips, enormous Easter baskets, delicious dinners on Sundays, and who could forget her world-famous apple pies? I sat thinking and crying and reminiscing.

On that sunny, sad day in Savannah, Georgia, I walked to the front of the church and gave a speech beginning with these words:

"I'm Markiesha Wilson, Laraine's youngest daughter. My mother taught me how to be a Christian, how to be a strong Black woman, and how to be a flirt. She insisted that all her children and grandchildren were hard-working, well-educated, independent, and successful, because she was. She gave me her sense of humor, love for the beach, big smile, and resilient spirit. I am grateful that Laraine Mary Wilson was my mother and I loved her very much."

When I took my seat on the front row, my soul was at peace. I learned my serenity was connected to my acceptance that my mother, with all her frailties, was the best mother she could be. She had made me who I was, flaws and all. I learned acceptance meant

I could forgive her though I would never hear an apology. I could forgive her for who she was and who she wasn't. I could forgive her for what she did and what she did not do. I found my serenity was completely aligned to my gratitude for her.

When I look back over my life, I can only feel grateful to God, the One who brought me through every situation. I agree with the apostle John who said in John 21:25 (NIV), "Jesus did many other things as well. If every one of them were written down, I suppose that even the whole world would not have room for the books that would be written."

EMBRACING SERENITY @ WORK

Acceptance, forgiveness, and gratitude are secrets to finding serenity in life and in the workplace.

First, accept some truths about work. Work is a place you go to make money and pay your expenses. Period. While you may make lifelong friends there, your primary purpose is to do a job. With this perspective, you can understand and accept that people at work are motivated toward their own success. This is not to say all co-workers are evil people who are out to get you, but neither should you expect them to put your aspirations above their own.

Next, accept that whether or not they have hostile intent, your co-workers' movements will be dictated by their own goals. We can find peace at work when we accept that co-workers and bosses are people first.

Work is part of your life, but it is not your whole life. Spending more than eight hours a day with the same people creates many opportunities for misunderstandings, miscommunications, and offenses to occur. It is almost impossible to avoid these challenges in the workplace. To achieve a place of peace, forgive—forgive co-workers and managers for overtalking you in meetings; for throwing you under the bus to avoid being found out or held responsible; and for not valuing your time and talent.

Being grateful for being gainfully employed is a critical element of the serenity secret sauce. Gratitude for the gifts and talents you possess to do your job are the foundation for appreciating what you have. Moreover, being grateful for the lessons you've learned, no matter what challenges the workplace has thrown your way, can help you reach a place of peace.

During a particularly challenging season in 2019, I decided to express my gratitude for my leaders. Here's what I posted on social media:

> *"In this season of Thanksgiving, I feel compelled to express my gratitude to the remarkable women who have nurtured my career. I have enjoyed over a twenty-year professional journey in management consulting*

firms and financial institutions full of high-powered men, and yet have had the extraordinarily good fortune to have only worked for women managers and senior leaders. Let me say upfront that this is not a hashtag anything anti-male post, (I LOVE men), but rather a celebration of the privilege I have enjoyed working under only women.

"I am grateful for all the lessons I learned from you women—both those that were painful and those that were joyful. Thank you critiquing and celebrating my creativity. Thank you for hushing and highlighting my humor. Thank you advising my ambition to climb the corporate ladder and accommodating my addiction to pursue planes bound for the tropics. Thank you for polishing and praising my work performance. Thank you for supporting and safeguarding my single-parenting of my niece. Thank you for never belittling, but always boosting my Blackness.

"Thank you to Angel, Louise, Elizabeth, Debra, Judy, Jean, Olga, Kristi, Carol, Aida, Lisa S., Patty, Haritha, Raquel, Nicole, Shannon and Lisa T. I count you all as members of a very exclusive club of phenomenal women who have impacted me in ways you'll never fully know. I hope it is enough to say that you have made me the leader I am today, and I am eternally grateful for each and every one of you."

In all my living, working, parenting, and learning, I believe having peace is the most important part of achieving success, thriving in my career, and finding joy in living.

"And we know that in
all things God works for
the good of those who
love him, who have been
called according to his
PURPOSE."
Romans 8:28 (NIV)

Take Your Step

ASK YOURSELF

Who do you need to accept, forgive, and show gratitude for?

TASK YOURSELF

Stop procrastinating. Contact them this week.

Herstorical Fact

OPRAH WINFREY, a philanthropist, media mogul, and actress has enjoyed a lifetime of success—but only after forgiving those who hurt her. Oprah suffered from sexual abuse from family members and emotional abuse from her mother. Yet as she moved through life, she found forgiveness was the key to her peace. She talks often about her favorite definition of forgiveness from Dr. Gerald G. Jampolsky who said, "It is about letting go of our perception that we need to hold a grievance for the rest of our lives.... It's really about letting go of the past we thought we wanted. We can't really change that past."[15] Oprah accepted this principle, and it has led her to experience freedom and serenity.

As one of the most successful women of our time, Oprah credits her ability to forgive as the key to living her best life. Forgiveness is certainly linked to finding serenity.

Chapter 9

Ending with Joy

Trust God always and pursue joy.

PHILIPPIANS 4 IS MY FAVORITE chapter of the entire Bible. In only twenty-three verses, it explains how to stay encouraged, get along with others, and maintain peace of mind. The apostle Paul wrote this book to encourage and instruct the church when was he was in prison.

While I am not in prison and am now in fact feeling freer than ever before, I would like to take this final opportunity to leave you with my encouraging words. If I was asked to write the Markiesha International Version (MIV) of Philippians 4, it would sound like this:

Therefore, my brothers and sisters, you whom I hope and pray the best for, I urge you to look to God for everything you need and look to each other for the love you want.

I encourage you to support every single person you can. Help them professionally, financially, emotionally, and spiritually. Instead of spending time feeling bad for or critiquing someone's situation, do something about it. Share your resources to equip the people around you to become better and live their best lives. Maybe you can't change the whole world, but you can impact the people in your sphere of influence.

Spend your mind wisely. Focus on the positive you see all around you—not the negative. Do not waste time worrying. Instead, spend that time praying. You will have peace if you remember to pray to God when you are in troubling situations.

I plead with all humans of all shades, races, religions, genders, and sexual orientations to stop quarreling and spewing hate at one another. God sees us all as human and loves every one of us. He doesn't love any group more than another. Be intentional about doing the same. Stop hating and hurting each other just because you look, act, or think different. Instead, love each other because you were all made in the image of the same God.

On my tough journey to joy, I have learned to be

content whatever my circumstances. I know what it feels like to be in need, and I know what it feels like to have abundance. I have learned the secret of being content in every situation, whether I've got money in the bank, food in the fridge, good or bad credit. The secret is I can do everything with God who is the source of my strength.

In these chapters, I've shared my struggles, stories, and strategies. What you have learned, put it into practice as soon as possible. Set aside time to plan when and how you will take these audacious steps in your climb. Don't wait or procrastinate. Tomorrow is not promised.

In my climb, I have been blessed with extraordinary colleagues, employees, managers, and clients at amazing companies who helped me find each step forward. I am grateful for every experience and person who supported me at Towson University, Booz Allen and Hamilton, Fannie Mae, First Bank Virgin Islands, ITT/Excelis, Accenture, and Deloitte. The remarkable gifts you gave me enabled, equipped, and empowered me to create my own company, WilsonChapman™ and Associates. Thank you and may God bless you!

Finally know this, God promises us all an abundant life of peace and joy if we believe. His timing is perfect. It is never one millisecond early or late. Trust God always and pursue joy.

Bibliography

1. Meriam-Webster, s.v. "endurance," accessed June 6, 2021, http://merriam-webster.com/dictionary/endurance
2. Shinn, Florence. *The Wisdom of Florence Scovel Shinn. Your Word is Your Wand.* First Fireside Edition. New York. DeVorss & Company. 1989.
3. X, Malcolm. "Speech on the Founding of the OAAU June 28, 1964." Thinkingtogether.org. Last modified May 25, 2021. http://www.thinkingtogether.org/rcream/archive/Old/S2006/comp/OAAU.pdf
4. LifeWay Staff. "Spiritual Gifts Survey (Discovery Tool)". Lifeway.com. September 10, 2015.https://www.lifeway.com/en/articles/women-leadership-spiritual-gifts-growth-service
5. Downer-McCoy, Sheila. *Shape* (*Strategically Helping Another Person Elevate*). BookBaby. 2021.
6. Melaku, Tsedale, Angie Beeman, David G. Smith, and W. Brad Johnson. "Be a Better Ally." *Harvard Business Review.* November – December 2020. https://hbr.org/2020/11/be-a-better-ally.
7. Bradberry, Travis and Jean Greaves. *Emotional Intelligence 2.0.* San Diego, CA: Talent Smart 2009.
8. Cambridge Dictionary, s.v. "audacity," accessed June 9, 2021, http://dictionary.cambridge.org/dictionary/learner-english/audacity.
9. Page, Susan. "Read the full transcript of vice presidential debate between Mike Pence and Kamala Harris."usatoday.com. Last modified October 8, 2020. https://www.usatoday.com/story/news/politics/elections/2020/10/08/vice-presidential-debate-full-transcript-mike-pence-and-kamala-harris/5920773002/
10. Harris, Kamala. "Harris: You Ushered in a New Day for America."npr.org. November 7, 2020. https://www.npr.org/sections/live-updates-2020-election-results/2020/11/07/932646213/harris-you-ushered-in-a-new-day-for-america#transcript
11. Ulrich, Laurel Thatcher. *Well-Behaved Women Seldom Make History*. New York: Alfred A. Knopf. 2007.
12. Franken, Robert. *Human Motivation Sixth Edition*. Australia: Thomas-Wadsworth. 2007.
13. Hinckley, David. "Cicely Tyson 1924 – 2021." RSS, January 29, 2021. http://www.tvworthwatching.com/post/Cicely-Tyson-1924-2021.aspx.
14. Sisavat, Monica. Legendary Icon Cicely Tyson Dies at 96: "Her Power and Grace Will Be With Us Forever", January 29, 2021. https://www.msn.com/en-us/lifestyle/lifestyle-buzz/legendary-icon-cicely-tyson-dies-at-96-her-power-and-grace-will-be-with-us-forever/ss-BB1dbZbe.
15. Oprah's Forgiveness Aha! Moment | Oprah's Life Class | Oprah Winfrey Network. YouTube. YouTube, 2011. https://m.youtube.com/watch?v=Rwcp_oElwnU.

"The cover was inspired by Markiesha Wilson's life story. Markiesha has been a role model in my life since I was a young girl, so I was thrilled to take on this commission as I have personal ties to several symbols in the artwork. Each flower represents a person from Markiesha's past, present, and legacy. The painting reflects her journey and development as a leader, mother, friend, and daughter. I am honored to have been able to execute this project and I am excited to continue witnessing Markiesha's excellence."

—Saudia Jones, artist

ABOUT THE ARTIST

SAUDIA JONES is a New York-based mixed media artist from St. Thomas, VI. She received her BFA from The New School and is working in art administration. Her work is primarily centered around family, childhood memories, and storytelling.

Contact:
flolisjewels.com
jones.saudia@gmail.com

About the Author

Management Consultant and Leadership Coach, **MARKIESHA E. WILSON,** has spent her entire career encouraging her clients, teams, and colleagues to build work environments and careers that energize them. In this inspirational manual, Markiesha shares the techniques she learned and applied to help her strategically navigate necessary nonsense in the workplace, excel in leadership roles at Fortune 500 companies, and heal from her troubled past and personal challenges.